Practise

Reading Comprehension

KS2 ENGLISH

Age 7–9

Brenda Stones

Advice for parents

We are surrounded by things to read: billboards, adverts, circulars, websites, newspapers and, finally, books. The skill we need to develop is how to be a critical reader: to think about where all this stuff is coming from, who wrote it and why, and which pieces we should respond to and how.

This book presents a range of the real kinds of reading that we encounter, and helps children start to sift and sort, skim and scan, so that they develop a better understanding of how to read.

The questions are similar in style to the National Tests (the SATs):

- Multiple choice questions 1–2, for the child to select a quick answer
- Short answer questions 3–4, for short phrases of answers
- Long answer question 6, for a more reflectively written sentence
- Final question 7, often about the child's personal response to the text.

The '**How have I done?**' section invites your child to revisit the texts and to summarise their findings.

Finally, the answers section gives guidance on how to be a critical reader of each of the texts in the book.

The key difference to the National Tests is that in this book we're not looking for right answers: this is a practice book, not a test book, so we're prompting children to ask the right questions, to learn the process of reading, rather than come up with predicted answers that can be marked. After all, it's only year 3 or 4 of primary school: this is the time to learn how to read, understand and enjoy, before you need worry too much about getting the right answers!

Every effort has been made to trace all copyright holders, but if any have been inadvertently overlooked, the publisher will be pleased to make the necessary arrangements at the first opportunity.

First published 2007
exclusively for WHSmith by
Hodder Education, an Hachette UK company
338 Euston Road
London
NW1 3BH

Impression number   10 9 8 7 6 5 4 3
Year   2010
Text and illustrations © Hodder Education 2007

Cover illustration: Sally Newton Illustrations
Character illustrations: Beehive Illustration
All other illustrations: Simon Dennett at SD Illustration, Arthur Pickering and Kelly Gray
Typeset by Florence Production Ltd, Stoodleigh, Devon

ISBN   978 0340 94341 0

Printed and bound in Italy

Contents

Welcome to Kids Club!

Hi, readers. My name's Charlie and I run Kids Club with my friend Abbie. Kids Club is an after-school club which is very similar to one somewhere near you.

We'd love you to come and join our club and see what we get up to!

I'm Abbie. Let's meet the kids who will work with you on the activities in this book.

My name's Jamelia. I look forward to Kids Club every day. The sports and games are my favourites, especially on Kids Camp in the school holidays.

Hi, I'm Megan. I've made friends with all the kids at Kids Club. I like the outings and trips we go on the best.

Hello, my name's Kim. Kids Club is a great place to chill out after school. My best friend is Alfie – he's a bit naughty but he means well!

I'm Amina. I like to do my homework at Kids Club. Charlie and Abbie are always very helpful. We're like one big happy family.

Greetings, readers, my name's Alfie! Everybody knows me here. Come and join our club; we'll have a wicked time together!

Now you've met us all, tell us something about yourself.
All the kids filled in a '**Personal Profile**' when they joined. Here's one for you to complete.

Personal Profile

Name: _____

Age: _____

School: _____

Home town: _____

Best friend: _____

My favourite:

- Book _____
- Film _____
- Food _____
- Sport _____

My hero is _____ because _____

_____

When I grow up I want to be a _____

If I ruled the world the first thing I would do is _____

_____

If I could be any celebrity for a day I would be _____

_____

1: Advert

This is part of an advert sent through the post by one of the supermarkets.

Our Taste the difference 'slow baked' all butter cookies are baked for longer at a lower temperature to make them wonderfully crumbly.

Try heating Taste the difference chocolate cookies in a pan then packing the mixture into a cake tin. Mix two pots of strawberries and cream yogurt with two packs of soft cheese, spoon over the base and chill.

Oooh, what's that over there?

Let's practise

1 How many different kinds of type are used in this part of the advert?

One ☐   Two ☐   Three ☐

2 Tick all the kinds of illustration used.

Photograph ☐   Cartoon ☐   Map ☐

3 Why does this supermarket think their cookies are better than other people's?

_____

_____

4 What is the purpose of the second paragraph?

_____

_____

5 How many ingredients would you need?

_____

6 What is this advert trying to persuade you to do?

_____

7 What might be the purpose of the person in the cartoon?

_____

2: List

This is a list of rides from the Alton Towers website.

Choose your DAY and place to STAY...
and let the fun begin...

play-and-stay.co.uk

Home | Opening Times | Ride Guide | Seasonal Events | Ride Restrictions | F.A.Q's | Terms | Contact Us

ZONE RIDE GUIDE

Alton Towers is one of the UK's biggest and most popular theme parks. It has been split up into numerous zones and areas, each of which offering fun and excitement.

ALTON TOWERS ZONES

ADVENTURE LAND
Rides for all the family that really capture the imagination – home of the Spinball Whizzer.

CRED STREET
Shows and rides for younger children and home of the Tweenies!

FORBIDDEN VALLEY
Only the brave should enter the Forbidden Valley, home of the mighty Air, Nemesis, Ripsaw and Blade.

GLOOMY WOOD
Brave the spooks and take on the dead in Duel.

KATANGA CANYON
Rise to the call of the wild and ride the Congo River Rapids.

MERRIE ENGLAND
Take it easy on the teacups or prepare for saturation at the hands of The Flume.

OLD MACDONALD'S FARMYARD
All the fun of the farm – singalongs and tractor rides await younger children and families.

THE TOWERS
Investigate The Legend of the Towers with Hex

UG LAND
Primal force and thrills in UG Land with Rita – Queen of Speed

X-SECTOR
High-tech adventures await you in the X-Sector – Fall into Oblivion and give in to Submission.

< (BOOK NOW!) (Back)

www.play-and-stay.co.uk - Book Online Now or Call Our Specialist Call Centre Team on **0800 9555 980**
Contact Us Regarding Theme Park Packages - E-Mail:**admin-play-and-stay@holidayextras.com**

Let's practise

1 You would find this page:

in a magazine ☐

in a newspaper ☐

on screen ☐

2 This page is listing:

hotels ☐   safari parks ☐   rides ☐

3 In what order are the rides listed?

_____

4 Which rides are recommended for younger children?

_____

5 Which sound like the scariest rides?

_____

6 What action is the website asking you to take next?

_____

_____

7 How could you improve the last sentence of the introduction?

_____

_____

Here is a page about a special event from London Zoo's website.

ZSL The Zoological Society of London

Dates: 21 – 29 Oct
Times: All Day

Face your fears at London Zoo this Halloween, with a half-term packed full of spine-tingling activities.

Get your adrenaline pumping in our interactive Halloween Spectacular show and discover which animals hide, spit or change colour when confronted by what terrifies them most.

Visit our starlit den to hear hair-raising tales of ghostly goings on at the Zoo. Conjure up a fiendish 'finger bat' or a monstrous mask in our Halloween-themed workshops!

Don't miss your chance to learn about the darker side of animal behaviour in our Halloween-themed Animals in Action demonstration.

Book your tickets online and save 10%.

- Storytelling sessions will run at 12pm, 2pm and 4pm

Find more events at London Zoo

RSS News Feed
© Copyright ZSL 2007

Let's practise

1 The Zoological Society is:

a library ☐

a zoo ☐   a circus ☐

2 Which season is being celebrated?

Christmas ☐   Hallowe'en ☐   New Year ☐

3 **Alliteration** means repeating letters for effect, like 'frightening fun'. Can you find four more examples?

_____

_____

4 List four adjectives which add to the spooky atmosphere:

_____

_____

5 List four activities that are on offer:

_____

_____

6 Who is this bit of the website addressed to, and how can you tell?

_____

7 How do you think the photograph was taken?

_____

If you want to find out some facts about Hallowe'en, you might look it up on the online encyclopedia, Wikipedia.

Halloween

A jack-o'-lantern

Also called	**Hallowe'en**, All Hallows Eve, All Saints' Eve, Samhain, Spooky Day, Snap-Apple Night, Costume Day/Día de los Disfrazes, and Pooky Night
Observed by	Many English-speaking nations, including the USA, Ireland, Scotland, Wales, England, Canada, sometimes Australia and New Zealand
Type	Religious, Cultural (celebrated mostly irrespective of religion)
Significance	There are many sources of Halloween's significance
Date	October 31
Celebrations	Trick-or-treating, Bobbing for apples, Costume parties, Carving jack-o'-lanterns

Halloween or **Hallowe'en** is a tradition celebrated on the night of October 31, most notably by children dressing in costumes and going door-to-door collecting sweets, fruit, and other gifts. Apart from this trick-or-treating, there are many other traditional Halloween activities. Some of these include costume parties, watching horror films, going to "haunted" houses, and traditional autumn activities such as hayrides, some of these even "haunted".

Halloween originated under a different name ("Samhain") as a Pagan festival among the Celts of Ireland and Great Britain with mainly Irish and Scots and other immigrants transporting versions of the tradition to North America in the nineteenth century. Most other Western countries have embraced Halloween as a part of American pop culture in the late twentieth century.

1 What is the date of Hallowe'en?

October 13 ☐   October 31 ☐

October 11 ☐

2 What was its original name?

Samhain ☐   Spooky Day ☐

All Hallows Eve ☐

3 What does the photo show?

_____

4 There are apostrophes in Hallowe'en and jack-o'-lantern for missing letters. Which letters?

_____

5 What does the text say that children do on Hallowe'en?

_____

_____

6 Where did the tradition start?

_____

_____

7 How is the text laid out in the two different panels?

_____

This is what to do on Bonfire Night, to keep your pets safe.

TOP TIPS

Make sure your pets are safe by following RSPCA advice:

- Keep dogs and cats indoors at night (exercise your dog during the day).

- Close windows, curtains, play music or turn up the TV to drown out the noise.

- Let your pets take refuge under furniture or in a corner if they wish. Don't try to tempt them out as this may cause further stress.

- Make sure your pets are microchipped or wearing an identity disc in case they go missing.

- Ask your vet about the Dog Appeasing Pheromone, which calms dogs down.

- Bring small animals such as rabbits and guinea pigs indoors.

- Finally, always remember to check your bonfire pile before lighting it in case hedgehogs or other wildlife have crawled underneath.

Let's practise

1 This list of Top Tips is:

a recipe ☐

instructions from the RSPCA ☐

map directions ☐

2 The list is arranged by:

numbers ☐

alphabetically ☐

bullet points ☐

3 Should you keep your pets in a quiet environment?

_____

4 Which animals should you check for, as well as your pets?

_____

5 Which hi-tech developments can now help pets?

_____

6 What do you think the RSPCA would really prefer to happen?

_____

_____

7 List the imperative verbs in this list of instructions.

_____

_____

This is a newspaper article that discusses how best to feed the birds.

BIRD FEEDING TIPS

Feeding bread to birds in parks may seem like a good idea, but it can harm them.

Bread gets mouldy quickly and mould can give birds breathing problems. Stale food also breeds salmonella and other bacteria, which can poison birds.

Recently, 40 swans, ducks and geese were found dead at a pond in Snaresbrook and it is feared they were poisoned by food left by visitors.

You should use bird seed mixtures available from supermarkets, garden centres and pet outlets instead. Specialist bird foods are also available such as bird cake and live insects. Other good foods include cooked unsalted rice, suet, mild tasting grated cheese and cooked or raw pastry.

Let's practise

1 This article is:

a list of ingredients ☐

a point of view ☐

an advert ☐

2 What caused the birds to die?

Vandals ☐   Poisoned water ☐   Mouldy and/or stale food ☐

3 Why may bread not be a good food for birds?

_____

4 What does the writer of the article want us to buy for the birds from shops?

_____

5 What foods can we still use from home?

_____

6 Does the article believe the visitors to the park intended to poison the birds?

_____

7 How does the first paragraph lead us in?

_____

_____

7: Explanation

This is a newspaper article explaining what to do about flu.

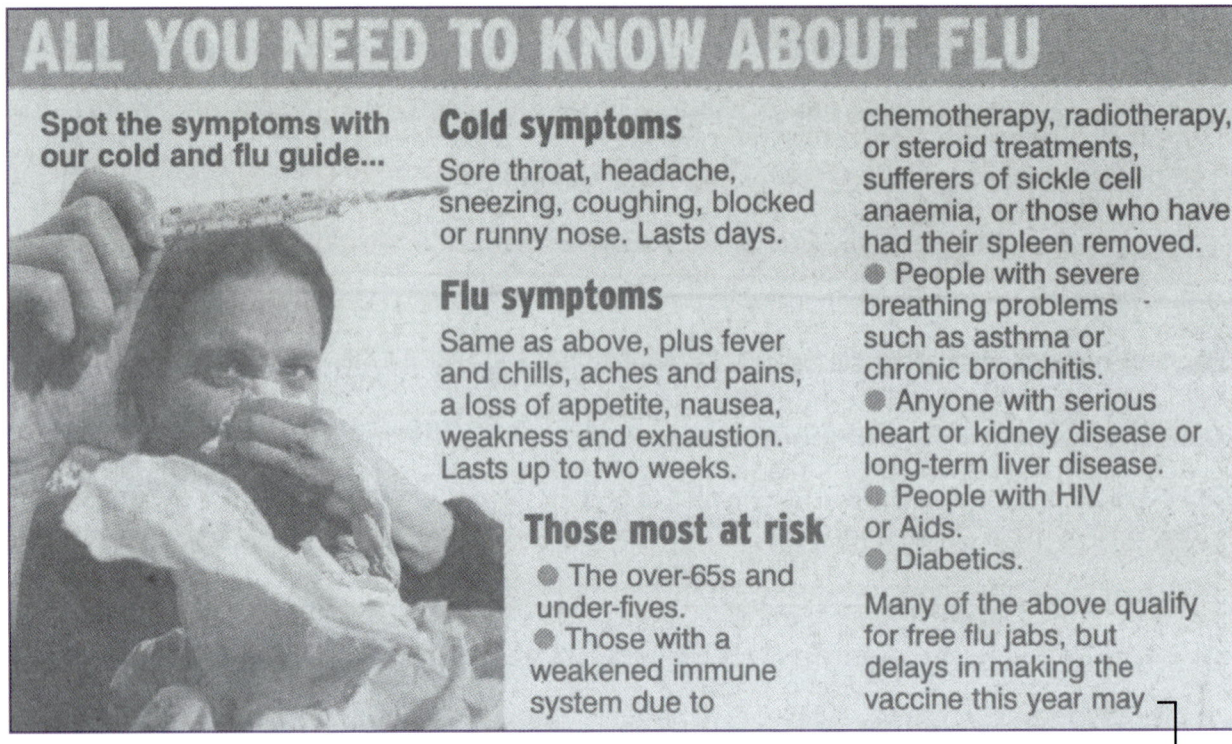

ALL YOU NEED TO KNOW ABOUT FLU

Spot the symptoms with our cold and flu guide...

Cold symptoms

Sore throat, headache, sneezing, coughing, blocked or runny nose. Lasts days.

Flu symptoms

Same as above, plus fever and chills, aches and pains, a loss of appetite, nausea, weakness and exhaustion. Lasts up to two weeks.

Those most at risk

- The over-65s and under-fives.
- Those with a weakened immune system due to chemotherapy, radiotherapy, or steroid treatments, sufferers of sickle cell anaemia, or those who have had their spleen removed.
- People with severe breathing problems such as asthma or chronic bronchitis.
- Anyone with serious heart or kidney disease or long-term liver disease.
- People with HIV or Aids.
- Diabetics.

Many of the above qualify for free flu jabs, but delays in making the vaccine this year may mean a wait of a few weeks. Check with your GP.

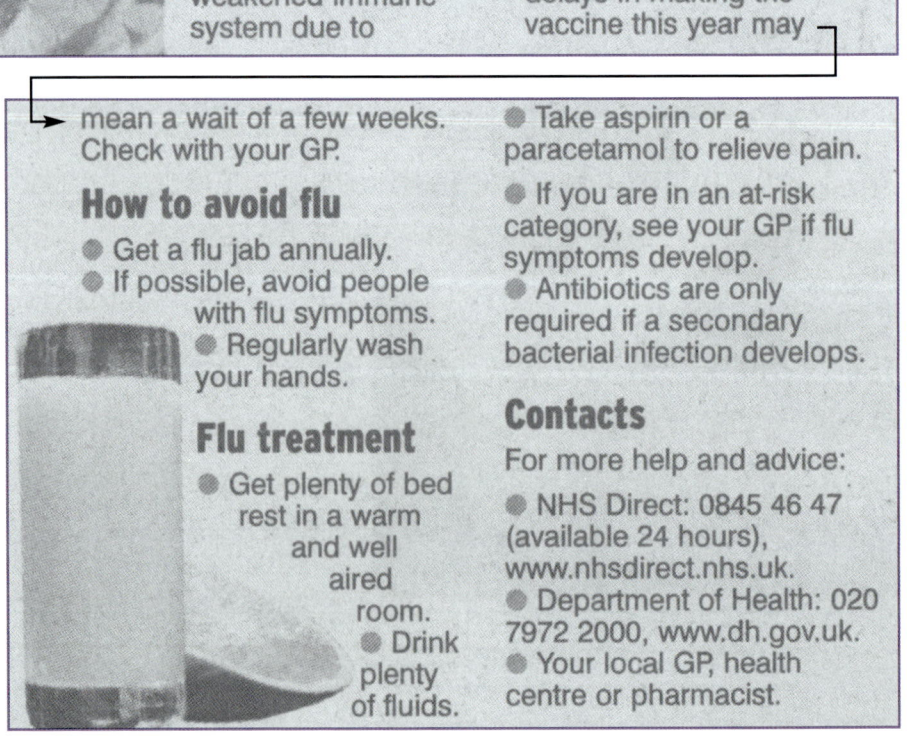

How to avoid flu

- Get a flu jab annually.
- If possible, avoid people with flu symptoms.
- Regularly wash your hands.

Flu treatment

- Get plenty of bed rest in a warm and well aired room.
- Drink plenty of fluids.
- Take aspirin or a paracetamol to relieve pain.
- If you are in an at-risk category, see your GP if flu symptoms develop.
- Antibiotics are only required if a secondary bacterial infection develops.

Contacts

For more help and advice:

- NHS Direct: 0845 46 47 (available 24 hours), www.nhsdirect.nhs.uk.
- Department of Health: 020 7972 2000, www.dh.gov.uk.
- Your local GP, health centre or pharmacist.

Let's practise

1 The person in the photo is:

looking at a thermometer ▢

covering her head ▢

lifting a pencil ▢

2 The article is written in:

the first person ('we') ▢

the second person ('you') ▢

the third person ('they') ▢

3 How much longer does flu last than a cold?

_____

4 What activity can you easily do to avoid flu?

_____

5 What are the two reasons to contact your doctor (GP)?

_____

_____

6 What features in the article make it easy to absorb the information?

_____

_____

7 Who do you think gave the newspaper the information for the article?

_____

This newspaper article puts reasons for and against women being bus drivers.

WANTED: Women with drive

ONLY 6 PER CENT of all of London's thousands of bus drivers are women, figures show.

Of the capital's 22,000 bus drivers just 1,300 are women – even though women make up more than half of London's population.

Now Mayor Ken Livingstone has called for more women to apply for jobs as bus drivers in an effort to make the profession more representative.

He said: 'The majority of Londoners are women and the majority of bus trips are made by women. Only when the make–up of bus companies' staff better reflects this will bus operators truly understand the needs of the majority of its passengers.

'Many women might think it's too difficult to drive a bus, particularly the double-deckers. But buses are far easier to drive these days. Power steering and better designs mean that if you are strong enough to drive a car, you are strong enough to drive a bus.

'Bus companies are also becoming more flexible in their work patterns. Though policies may vary, many garages now offer shift patterns that fit more easily into family life.'

1 How many bus drivers are there in London:

1300 ☐

22,000 ☐

6 per cent ☐

2 How many are women:

22,000 ☐

half ☐

6 per cent ☐

3 Who wants more women to be bus drivers?

_____

4 Why did the newspaper choose this headline for the article?

_____

5 What three reasons are given for why women should apply for the job?

a _____

b _____

c _____

6 What reason is given for why women might not be applying for the job?

_____

7 What would be your reasons for and against being a bus driver?

For: _____

Against: _____

Here is how another woman chose her particular job. This biography comes from the publisher's website for Lauren Child, who wrote the Clarice Bean books.

The Watts Publishing Group. Orchard Books, Lauren Child Information page

http://www.wattspub.co.uk/lchilob.htm

Q▾ Google

Search engines ▾   Simon's favourites ▾   Rally stuff ▾   Sport ▾   Phone and Games ▾   Clipart ▾   Macintosh ▾   Mac Maintenance ▾   Tutorials ▾

Author Information

Lauren Child

Lauren Child grew up in Wiltshire as the middle child of three sisters and the daughter of two teachers. She has always been interested in the many aspects of childhood, from gazing into toy shop windows to watching American children's shows from the 1960s. After attending two Art Schools, where Lauren admits that she did not learn much, she travelled for six months, still unsure about which career to embark upon.

Before Lauren started writing and illustrating children's books she started her own company 'Chandeliers for the People' making exotic, elegant lampshades. It was only when she came to write and illustrate the book **Clarice Bean, That's Me** that she decided to devote her time to writing and illustrating books for children, which combines her fascination for childhood and her talent for designing and creating. Lauren gets her inspiration from other people's conversations or from seeing something funny happen.

1. How many sisters did Lauren Child have?

   One ☐   Two ☐   Three ☐

2. What were her parents?

   Artists ☐

   Teachers ☐

   Lampshade makers ☐

3. Did she have any training in art?

   _____

4. Did she always know what she wanted to work at?

   _____

5. How does she get her ideas for what her characters say?

   _____

6. Do you think there's any link between designing lampshades and illustrating books?

   _____

7. Can you think of any other authors who illustrate as well as write their books?

   _____

Here is a page from a book that Lauren Child wrote and illustrated, *Utterly Me, Clarice Bean*.

When I get downstairs, the whole kitchen is full of a bad mood. Marcie won't talk to Mum, and Kurt won't talk to Marcie. Grandad isn't talking to anyone because he hasn't plugged himself into his hearing-aid. Minal is talking to me but I wish he wouldn't. Minal is a niggling gnat and I have to have him sleeping in my room. Sometimes, when I want to keep him out, I pile lots of gubbins against the door. He is five.

Who wants to share a room with a five-year-old brother? I don't even need a five-year-old brother. I already have one who is a teenager called Kurt and that is enough brothers for anyone.

1. How many people are there in the kitchen?

   Five ☐   Six ☐   Seven ☐

2. How many people are talking?

   One ☐   Two ☐   Three ☐

3. Do you like the family being drawn sideways? Why?/Why not?

   _____

   _____

4. What does this do to the shape of the text?

   _____

5. What tense is the text written in, and why, do you think?

   _____

6. What is Clarice's opinion about brothers?

   _____

   _____

7. What do you feel about Grandad?

   _____

   _____

This is an interview with the author Terry Deary, best known for writing the *Horrible History* series.

Basics

Name
Terry Deary

Date of Birth
3 January 1946

Describe yourself in three words
Anti-establishment, anti-authority, angry

Childhood and School

Where did you grow up?
Sunderland, North East England

Education
Monkwearmouth School, Sunderland

What were you like at school?
Rebellious

What was your favourite subject?
Football

What was your worst subject?
Latin

What did you want to be when you grew up?
A footballer for Sunderland

Did you enjoy reading?
Wasn't offered the opportunity

What was your favourite book/author/type of book?
Read *Hotspur* and *Wizard* comics

Your Life Now

Where do you live?
Burnhope, Co. Durham

What is it like?
Former pit village, a bit rough

What is the best thing that has happened to you this year?
Completing a half-marathon in under two hours

Likes and Dislikes

What are your favourite pastimes?
Road running, reading, listening to music and supporting Sunderland Football Club

What are your favourite films/ TV programmes?
Old black and white movies

What do you most like about yourself?
Loyalty to my working class roots

What makes you cross?
Anything and everything

Writing

When did you first think about writing for a living?
At the age of 29

Which was your first book to be published?
The Custard Kid

Why do you write books?
I used to be an actor, performing popular children's plays. I decided to write those plays down as stories, and that's why I started. (I also like seeing my name on a book!)

Does writing come easily to you?
Writing is easy; being an author is very hard work

What do you do to get yourself in the mood for writing?
I sit in a small room in the roof of the house, where it's peaceful to work

Do you have a particular audience in mind when you start to write a book?
Children, any children, no matter what their backgrounds are

1. Terry comes from which part of England?

   The north east ☐   The south west ☐

   The north west ☐

2. How many years has he been writing?

   Ten years ☐   Twenty years ☐

   Thirty years or more ☐

3. Did he like reading books as a kid?

   _____

4. How many times does he mention football here?

   _____

5. What job did he do before writing?

   _____

6. Do you think you'd like him if you met him? Why?/Why not?

   _____

   _____

7. How good a runner is he?

   _____

This is a piece from 'The Enchanted Castle' by E. Nesbit, who also wrote *The Railway Children*.

The narrow passage ended in a round arch all fringed with ferns and creepers. They passed through the arch into a deep, narrow gully whose banks were of stones, moss-covered; and in the crannies grew more ferns and long grasses. Trees growing on the top of the bank arched across, and the sunlight came through in changing patches of brightness, turning the gully to a roofed corridor of goldy-green. The path, which was of greeny-grey flagstones where heaps of leaves had drifted, sloped steeply down, and at the end of it was another round arch, quite dark inside, above which rose rocks and grass and bushes.

"It's like the outside of a railway tunnel," said James.

"It's the entrance to the enchanted castle," said Kathleen.

Let's practise

1. Which colour describes the sunset?

   gold ☐

   goldy-green ☐

   greeny-grey ☐

2. Which colour describes the path?

   grey ☐   greeny-grey ☐   goldy-green ☐

3. Which plants are mentioned?

   _____

   _____

4. Which nouns are used to describe the ground outside?

   _____

5. Compare the archway they leave and the archway they come to.

   _____

6. What does James compare the archway to?

   _____

   _____

7. What do you imagine they might find through the final arch?

   _____

13: Historical novel

This is a page from *Walking with the Dead*, by Tim Bowler. It is about the disease of leprosy, and how people treated lepers, in the Middle Ages.

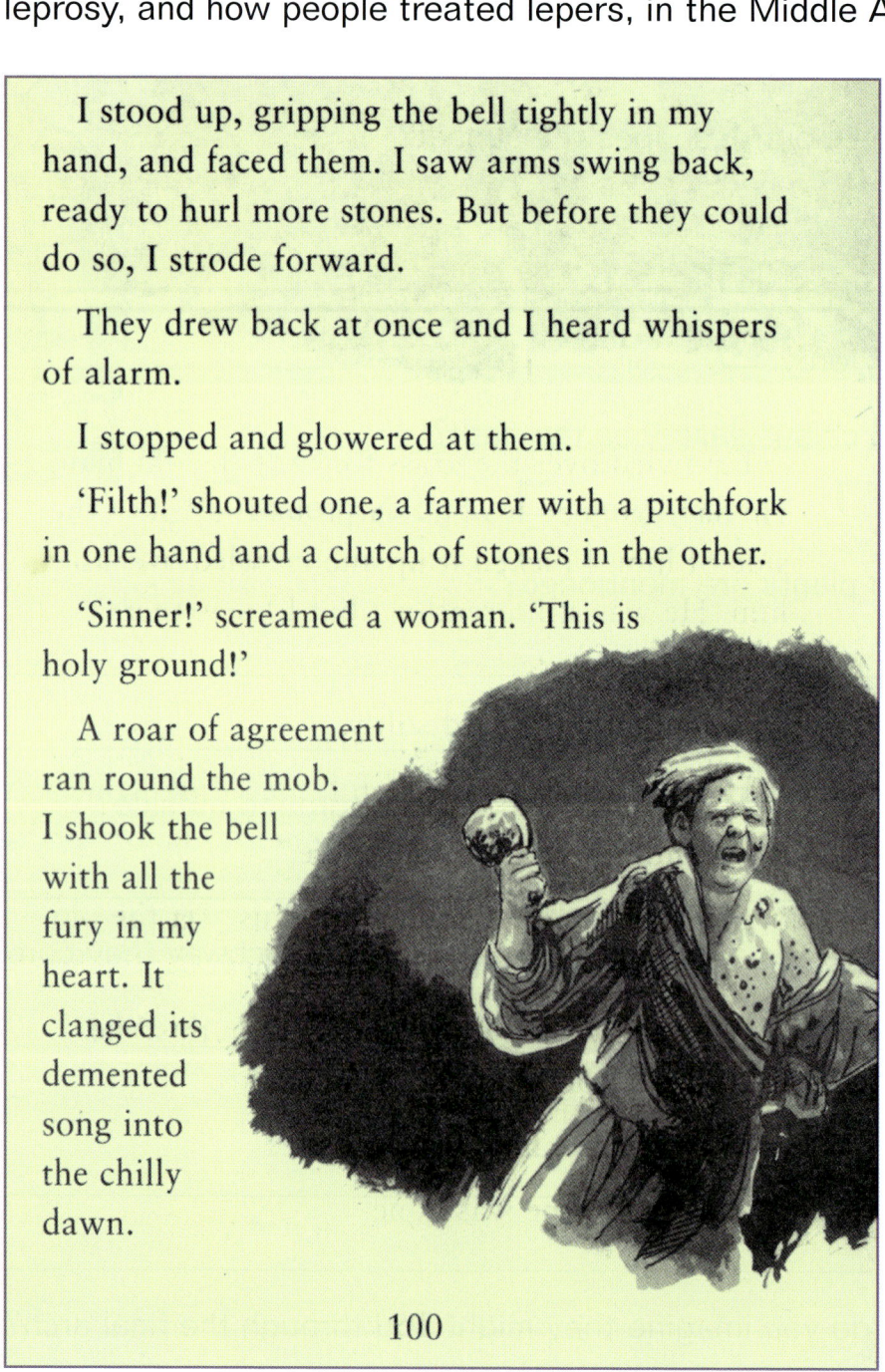

I stood up, gripping the bell tightly in my hand, and faced them. I saw arms swing back, ready to hurl more stones. But before they could do so, I strode forward.

They drew back at once and I heard whispers of alarm.

I stopped and glowered at them.

'Filth!' shouted one, a farmer with a pitchfork in one hand and a clutch of stones in the other.

'Sinner!' screamed a woman. 'This is holy ground!'

A roar of agreement ran round the mob. I shook the bell with all the fury in my heart. It clanged its demented song into the chilly dawn.

100

Let's practise

1 The time when this novel is set is:

the present day ☐   the Middle Ages ☐

the future ☐

2 What is the boy holding in his right hand?

A stone ☐   A bell ☐   A cup ☐

3 What clue is there to where this scene is happening?

_____

_____

4 What do the local people call lepers?

_____

5 What else are they about to do?

_____

6 Lepers had to ring a bell to warn people they were there. How does the boy use the bell in this scene?

_____

_____

7 What effect does the last sentence have, for you?

_____

_____

This is the first page of a play by Alan England.

The Killer Cave

---

1 Outside a cave in Derbyshire

Mr Weatherby, *a farmer, meets* **Harry**, **Joyce** *and* **Robbo**, *who are out looking for adventure during the summer holidays.* **Harry** *is clever and knows it,* **Joyce** *is a bit of a tomboy but sensible, and* **Robbo** *is a strong lad though slow on the uptake.*

Mr Weatherby: Hey! You can't go in there.

Harry: What?

Mr Weatherby: I said you can't go in that cave.

Harry: Why not? Do you live there, then?

   [**Robbo** *roars with laughter*]

Mr Weatherby: [*Pointing to a 'Danger: No Entry' sign*] There's rules.

Harry: I can read! Who's going to stop us, then?

Mr Weatherby: It's dangerous.

Joyce: Dangerous? Why?

Mr Weatherby: You'll get lost. A man got lost in that cave last year.

Let's practise

1 What is the setting for the opening of the play?

In a cave ☐   Outside a cave ☐

In Derby ☐

2 What children are there?

Two boys and a girl ☐   Three boys ☐

Four boys ☐

3 Who starts the talk between them all? Why?

_____

4 What is Robbo's part in the conversation?

_____

5 How do Harry's speeches show that he's 'clever and knows it'?

_____

_____

6 What clue are we given to what the rest of the play might be about?

_____

7 What do you think will happen next?

_____

This is the first page of a play by Peter Terson.

The Dividing Fence

---

1 The rear of a block of terraced houses

An open space without any hedges, walls or fences to show where each garden begins and ends. But the occupants know.
  The **Narrator** *enters.*

Narrator: When I was a youngster, during the war, we lived in a block. It was called 'the block', or 'our block'. It was a world of its own, and me and Brian Walker would play round the back of the block, or in the gardens of the block, chasing the Germans through the rhubarb. . . .

[*Two boys appear, standing on the path that runs from one end of the block to the other, passing all the back doors. They are outside number 3.* **Peter** *is the* **Narrator** *as a child.*]

Brian: Bet you daren't crawl through Gordon's garden.

Peter: Bet I dare.

Brian: Bet you daren't.

Peter: Bet I dare.

Let's practise

1 When does the play take place?

In the present day ▢

During the Second World War ▢

In the future ▢

2 How many actors are playing the part of Peter?

One ▢   Two ▢   Three ▢

3 Was there a 'dividing fence' during Peter's childhood?

_____

4 Were the Germans really hiding in the rhubarb?

_____

5 Who is the more taunting of the two children?

_____

6 Where do you think the action of the play will be centred?

_____

_____

7 Which of the two playscripts do you prefer? Why?

_____

_____

16: Poem about the senses

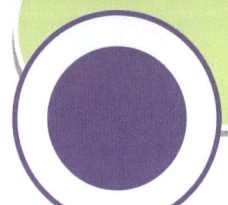

This poem was written by six-year-old children at Glyn-Corrwg Primary School in Glamorgan.

The Snowman

He shines like a candle
and melts slowly

He is white and black
and gets smaller all the time

He is as white as feathers
and white horses and snow

He glows in the dark
like a glow-worm

He stands on a flat place
and makes a shadow in the light

He crumples in a circle
like a circus tent

He turns to ice and slush
like a camel's hump

He runs away like milk
and melts like moonlight in sunshine

In the morning he has gone
like the moon

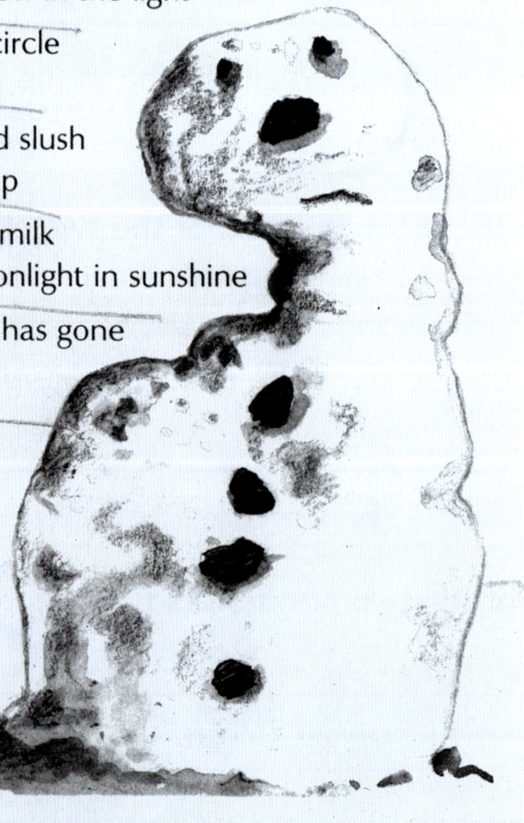

Let's practise

1. This poem is about:

   building a snowman ⬜

   watching it snow ⬜

   watching a snowman melt ⬜

2. It has:

   nine verses ⬜   three verses ⬜   one long verse ⬜

3. What is the snowman's colour compared to?

   _____

4. What is his brightness compared to?

   _____

5. What is the movement of his melting compared to?

   _____

   _____

6. Which do you think is the best comparison? Why?

   _____

   _____

7. What qualities of the snowman are similar to the moon?

   _____

17: Carnival poem

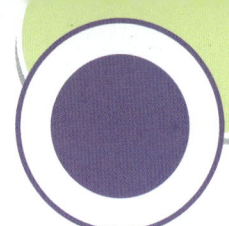

This is a poem by John Agard, who grew up in Guyana.

Tell me if ah seeing right
Take a look down de street

Words dancin
words dancin
till dey sweat
words like fishes
jumpin out a net
words wild and free
joinin de poetry revelry
words back to back
words belly to belly

Come on everybody
come and join de poetry band
dis is poetry carnival
dis is poetry bacchanal
when inspiration call
take yu pen in yu hand
if yu dont have a pen
take yu pencil in yu hand
if yu dont have a pencil
what the hell
so long de feeling start to swell
just shout de poem out

(extract from *Poetry Jump Up*)

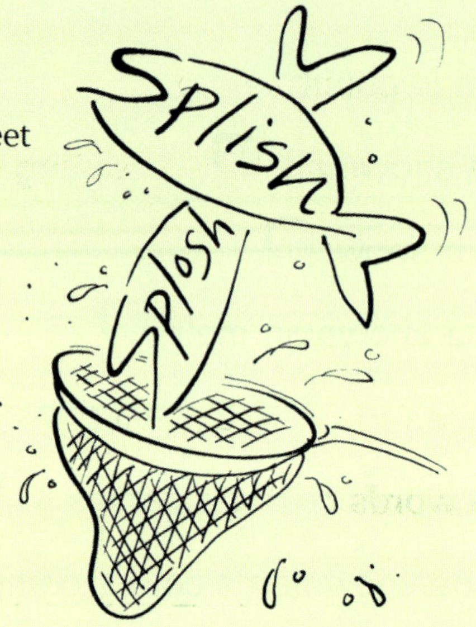

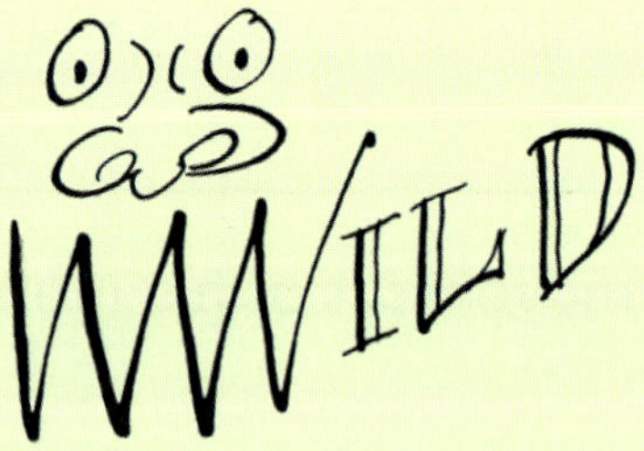

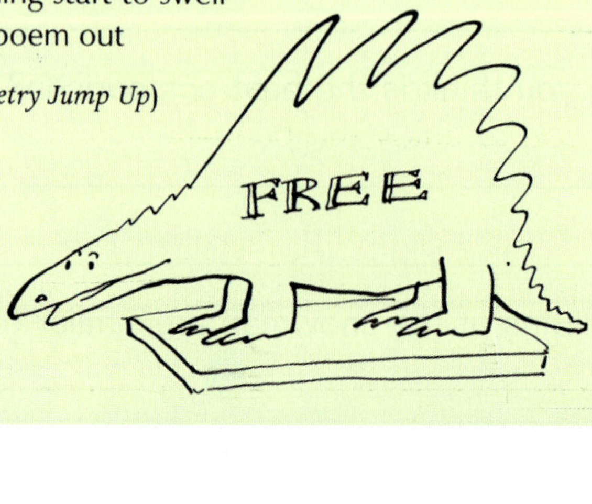

Let's practise

1 This poem should be read:

quietly to yourself ☐   shouting out loud ☐

in silence ☐

2 The dialect is from:

the Caribbean ☐   Scotland ☐   Australia ☐

3 What are words compared to?

_____

4 Which words and phrases does the poet repeat?

_____

_____

5 How does the rhythm develop through the poem?

_____

_____

6 Which is the line where the poet gives up with his word images, and just asks you to enjoy the poem?

_____

7 Which words have most fun in them, for you?

_____

Robert Louis Stevenson wrote many different kinds of fiction and travel books. He lived from 1850 to 1894.

Windy Nights

Whenever the moon and stars are set,
Whenever the wind is high,
All night long in the dark and wet,
A man goes riding by.
Late in the night when the fires are out,
Why does he gallop and gallop about?

Whenever the trees are crying aloud,
And ships are tossed at sea,
By, on the highway, low and loud,
By at the gallop goes he;
By at the gallop he goes, and then
By he comes back at the gallop again.

Robert Louis Stevenson

1   The main feature of this poem is:

rhythm ☐   humour ☐

characters ☐

2   The colours of the poem are:

dark ☑   bright ☐

multi-coloured ☒

3   Which lines rhyme?

_____

4   Which words and phrases are repeated?

_____

5   How does the poet manage to create the rhythm of the gallop?

_____

6   Do you think the rider really existed? Give your reasons.

_____

_____

7   Are there any signs that this poem was written so long ago?

_____

_____

How have I done?

1   **Who** were the authors or originators of the texts in this book?

Fill in the names and page numbers in the right columns.

Individual named writers	Organisations or companies
	p.6 Supermarket

2   **Why** were these texts written?

This time fill in the kinds of text and their page numbers.

For the reader to enjoy and learn	For the reader to take some action
	p.6 Advert

3 **Who** is the audience for each, do you think?

Mainly children	Mainly adults
	p.6 Supermarket

4 **How** are the texts laid out? Fill in what you remember for each piece!

Text	Features
p.6 Advert	2 separate paragraphs, photo and cartoon
p.8 List	
p.10 Website	
p.12 Information	
p.14 Instructions	
p.16 Discussion	
p.18 Explanation	
p.20 Newspaper article	
p.22 Children's author	
p.24 Family story	
p.26 Interview	
p.28 Mystery story	
p.30 Historical novel	
p.32 Playscript 1	
p.34 Playscript 2	
p.36 Poem about the senses	
p.38 Carnival poem	
p.40 Classic poem	

Answers

UNIT 1
1. Three
2. Photograph and cartoon
3. Because they're baked longer and more slowly
4. It's a recipe, to suggest extra foods you could go and buy.
5. Three: cookies, yogurts, soft cheese
6. To buy extra kinds of foods
7. To point you on to more different kinds of food

UNIT 2
1. On screen
2. Rides
3. Alphabetical order
4. Cred Street, Old Macdonald's Farmyard
5. Forbidden Valley, Gloomy Wood
6. Press the Book Now! button, or telephone, or e-mail.
7. each of which offers …

UNIT 3
1. A zoo
2. Hallowe'en
3. Face your fears, ghostly goings-on, monstrous mask, Animals in Action
4. starlit, spine-tingling, hair-raising, ghostly, fiendish, monstrous, darker
5. Storytelling, spectacular show, workshops, demonstrations
6. To both grown-ups and children, because it says 'you' to the child, but also includes booking information
7. With great care, in a safe room! It must have needed a specialised wildlife photographer to drape the snake over the pumpkin; the spider might have been added afterwards.

UNIT 4
1. October 31
2. Samhain
3. A pumpkin, or jack-o'-lantern
4. v from eve or evening; f from of the
5. Trick-or-treating
6. Ireland and Great Britain
7. On the right: 2 paragraphs of text; on the left: bold headings and notes

UNIT 5
1. Instructions from the RSPCA
2. Bullet points

3. No, you should actually turn up the noise at home to drown out the fireworks.
4. Hedgehogs and other wildlife that may be under the bonfire
5. Microchips and Dog Appeasing Pheromone
6. That people didn't have bonfires at home, and that there weren't any firework displays
7. Make sure, Keep, exercise, Close, play, turn up, Let, Don't try, Make sure, Ask, Bring, remember

UNIT 6
1. A point of view
2. Mouldy and/or stale food
3. It gets mouldy, which can give birds breathing problems.
4. Bird seed, bird cake, live insects
5. Cooked unsalted rice, suet, mild grated cheese, cooked or raw pastry
6. No, it thinks we are not aware of the dangers.
7. By saying that what we do now seems like a good idea, but if we read on we will get more information

UNIT 7
1. Looking at a thermometer
2. The second person ('you')
3. Over a week longer
4. Regularly wash your hands.
5. To see if there's a delay in getting a free flu jab; if you are in an at-risk category and you have symptoms
6. Bold headings for the things you need to know about, and bullet points to separate the different groups of at-risk people and the different things you need to do
7. The Department of Health and NHS Direct

UNIT 8
1. 22,000
2. 6 per cent
3. Mayor Ken Livingstone
4. To attract attention, like a Wanted poster. And to make a pun on 'drive', suggesting that women need energy to drive a bus.
5a. To represent the majority of passengers being women
  b. Buses are better designed, with power steering
  c. Flexible shift patterns fit into family life

6 Women might think double-deckers are difficult to drive
7 Personal answers, with reasons

UNIT 9
1 Two
2 Teachers
3 Yes, two different art colleges
4 No, she went travelling because she couldn't make up her mind.
5 She overhears people's conversations.
6 Yes, they both need a good eye for visual detail.
7 Quentin Blake, Anthony Browne, and many more

UNIT 10
1 Six
2 One
3 Yes or no, with any plausible reason
4 It means the left-hand margin of the text isn't straight; it bends round the illustrations.
5 The present tense, which makes it feel very immediate and close up
6 She really doesn't like either of her own brothers, and thinks one brother is enough for anyone.
7 Perhaps you feel sorry for Grandad, with the bird on his head?

UNIT 11
1 The north east
2 Thirty years or more
3 He didn't get the chance, but he liked reading comics.
4 Three times
5 He was an actor.
6 Yes or no, with any plausible reason
7 He must be pretty good to run a half-marathon at his age!

UNIT 12
1 Goldy-green
2 Greeny-grey
3 Ferns, creepers, moss, long grasses, trees, bushes
4 Gully, banks, stones, crannies, path, flagstones
5 Both are round arches. The one they leave is fringed with ferns and creepers. The one they come to has rocks, grass and bushes above it.

6 A railway tunnel
7 Use your imagination!

UNIT 13
1 The Middle Ages
2 A bell
3 The reference to 'holy ground' suggests that it's a churchyard.
4 'Filth!' and 'Sinner!'
5 Stone the boy
6 He shakes it hard to show his fury.
7 It's a very poetic sentence, after the stark language before.

UNIT 14
1 Outside a cave
2 Two boys and a girl
3 Mr Weatherby, to stop them going in the cave
4 Robbo just laughs.
5 He makes a joke about Mr Weatherby living in the cave; then he makes fun of the No Entry sign.
6 'You'll get lost', like the man last year . . .
7 Harry is bound to lead them into the cave . . .

UNIT 15
1 During the Second World War
2 Two
3 No, he remembers that they didn't need one then.
4 No, this was the children's imagination.
5 Brian is taunting Peter.
6 In the back gardens, before there were any dividing fences
7 Either one, backed up with a plausible reason

UNIT 16
1 Watching a snowman melt
2 Nine verses
3 Feathers, and white horses and snow
4 A candle, and a glow-worm
5 He crumples like a circus tent, and then runs away like milk.
6 Any of the comparisons in the poem (using 'like' or 'as'), with a plausible reason
7 He's gone in the morning.

UNIT 17
1 Shouting out loud
2 The Caribbean
3 'fishes jumpin out a net'

4   Words dancin; words (several times); come;
    dis is poetry; take yu pen/pencil in yu hand, if
    yu don't have
5   The lines get longer, so the rhythm becomes
    more involved.
6   'what the hell'
7   Maybe revelry, carnival, bacchanal – or any
    fun-sounding words or phrases from the poem

UNIT 18
1   Rhythm
2   Dark
3   Lines 1 with 3, 2 with 4, 5 with 6
4   Whenever; gallop and gallop; By; at the gallop
5   Much of the rhythm of the words is in triplets.
6   The title suggests he might be just the sound
    of the wind.
7   Not exactly, but some of the phrases like
    'fires are out' and 'on the highway' sound a
    bit historical.

How have I done?

1

Individual named writers	Organisations or companies
p.24 Lauren Child	p.6 Supermarket
p.28 E. Nesbit	p.8 Alton Towers/
p.30 Tim Bowler	play-and-stay
p.32 Alan England	p.10 Zoological
p.34 Peter Terson	Society of London
p.36 Class at	p.12 Wikipedia
Glyn-Corrwg	p.14 RSPCA
p.38 John Agard	p.16 Newspaper
p.40 Robert Louis	p.18 Newspaper/
Stevenson	NHS Direct/DoH
	p.20 Newspaper
	p.22 Publisher
	p.26 Magazine

2
You could make a slightly different choice, but
this is our suggested answer:

For the reader to enjoy and learn	For the reader to take some action
p.12 Information	p.6 Advert
p.22 Children's author	p.8 List
p.24 Family story	p.10 Website
p.26 Interview	p.14 Instructions
p.28 Mystery story	p.16 Discussion
p.30 Historical novel	p.18 Explanation
p.32 Playscript 1	p.20 Newspaper article
p.34 Playscript 2	
p.36 Poem about the senses	
p.38 Carnival poem	
p.40 Classic poem	

3

You could make a slightly different choice, but this is our suggested answer:

Mainly children	Mainly adults
p.24 Family story	p.6 Advert
p.28 Mystery story	p.8 List
p.30 Historical novel	p.10 Website
p.32 Playscript 1	p.12 Information
p.34 Playscript 2	p.14 Instructions
p.36 Poem about the senses	p.16 Discussion
p.38 Carnival poem	p.18 Explanation
p.40 Classic poem	p.20 Newspaper article
	p.22 Children's author
	p.26 Interview

4

Here are just a few:

Text	Features
p.6 Advert	Two separate paragraphs, photo and cartoon
p.8 List	Alphabetical list and photo
p.10 Website	Alliterative text and photo
p.12 Information	Encyclopedia entry, with main text and information box
p.14 Instructions	Bold heading and bullet points
p.16 Discussion	Bold heading and memo pad layout
p.18 Explanation	Bold heading, photos, subheadings, bullet points
p.20 Newspaper layout	Headline and narrow columns
p.22 Children's author	Photo and two paragraphs of text
p.24 Family story	Drawings up the side, and text curving round pictures
p.26 Interview	Q&A paragraphs, with photo
p.28 Mystery novel	Paragraph of description, followed by dialogue
p.30 Historical novel	Illustration and text
p.32 Playscript 1	Scene setting in italics, characters in bold
p.34 Playscript 2	Scene setting in italics, characters in bold
p.36 Poem about the senses	Verses of two lines, and illustration
p.38 Carnival poem	Verses getting longer, very few capitals, drawing
p.40 Classic poem	Two verses of six lines each

Sources